MW01658524

Praise for The CEO Clinician

"Cameisha has been such a great help and support as I have learned the behind the scenes of running an effective practice. It can be pretty vulnerable to ask for help and Cameisha provides such a safe space to help you navigate uncertainties."

- Sharita Bilson, LPC, Arkansas

"Before I started this program, I was dependent on social media for clients which was not consistent. I had no idea how to find my ideal clients in real life. Cameisha helped me come up with creative ways to get my name out there and find my ideal clients in day to day settings. I also hadn't thought of incorporating speaking into my business and now I have a concrete plan of how to do that. This not only creates additional income but also exposure to new referrals. I'm also thinking like a business owner now, not just like a therapist. I really benefited from Cameisha's guidance and appreciate how accessible she was throughout the process!"

-Lauren Walsh, LCSW, New Jersey

"I chose to work with Cameisha and invest in her coaching services because of her holistic and thorough approach, helping clinicians with every step of business ownership. While other coaches and consultants focus solely on marketing, Cameisha offers a program that focuses on marketing plus ALL the business logistics-- ALL of them. Her coaching program provides a step-by-step blueprint of how to open and operate a successful practice. I appreciate her ability to gently motivate and encourage you to step out and into the world as a proud business owner and clinician. Her program and coaching empowered me to accelerate opening my practice, to press that "publish" button on my website, and to confidently own my skills and market my business."

- Emily Dillon, LCSW, California

THE CEO CLINICIAN

SET UP, STRUCTURE, MARKET & SCALE YOUR MENTAL HEALTH PRIVATE PRACTICE IN 60 DAYS

CAMEISHA BREWER DICKERSON ED.S, LPC

ISBN 979-8-218-30786-8

Printed in the United States of America

Cover Design: Damascus Media
Photo:Cori Created Media
Editor: Miriam Arvinger, The Writing Expert

For more information please visit www.cbrewerconsulting.com and https://www.cbrewerconsulting.com/ceoclinicianbook

The CEO Clinician Book Bonus

Don't forget to visit https://www.cbrewerconsulting.com/ceoclinicianbookbonus to grab your bonus resources to support your reading experience.

Each chapter has a podcast episode reference. You can listen to the full episodes of The CEO Clinician Podcast here https://www.cbrewerconsulting.com/podcasts/the-ceo-clinician-podcast

Happy learning!

Thank you for your purchase. I cannot wait to work with you!

-Camiesha

DEDICATION

To my family and friends-thank you for giving me grace and space to write. Thank you for understanding my calling and being willing to share me with the world.

May God be glorified for all of the good things that will happen as a result of this book.

This book is for therapists who struggle to find hope and guidance in building a successful private practice. I wrote this book for the therapist who is ready to stop stressing about money every day and start doing meaningful clinical work.

Your new clients and your new lifestyle are waiting for you.

CONTENTS

INTRODUCTION

Welcome to the CEO Clinician: How to Set Up, Structure, Market & Scale Your Mental Health Private Practice in 60 Days. Thank you for purchasing this book. My prayer is that by the time you have finished reading, you will have clarity, confidence, and a deeper understanding of what it will take for you to build a private practice.

If you're reading this book, I already have an idea about the type of clinician that you are. You are probably the type of clinician who has a big heart, who desires to serve, and who wants to make sure that people get the mental health treatment they need. However, you have no clue how to approach the business side to make that happen. You may even be anxious, stressed out, questioning yourself, and wondering if you're cut out for this. You may even be going through cycles of self-sabotaging behavior. If you do the work and implement what I teach you through the framework of this book, these things will no longer be true about you.

So the purpose of this book is to serve as a guide for the new therapist just getting started in private practice with no business skills, no marketing skills, and no sales skills, but you're ready to make the transition from working for an agency to working in your private practice. The things that I will teach you will not be easy but they will be worth it.

I wish that I had this book when I started in private practice several years ago. I knew that I wanted to be in private practice. I didn't know what it would take, and I didn't know what it would require. But I knew that I couldn't stay where I was. I knew that I was an out-of-the-box therapist, meaning I wanted to do therapy creatively. I wanted to do things on my terms and my schedule with an uncapped income. It made no sense to sit around and wait every year for a couple of dollars an hour raise, even though I was technically salaried.

I struggled to build my private practice for a very long time. I made a lot of mistakes. If you're just getting started, at some point you will make mistakes too, but I'm here to help.

Let's do this!

PART 1

MINDSET OF A CEO CLINICIAN

CHAPTER 1:
SETTING YOUR MIND ON WHAT YOU WANT

Podcast Episode # 104 How to Set Up & Structure Your Private Practice

Before we begin there are a few things you need to know about me as the author. I have been exactly where you are. I used to be you. I used to be afraid of starting a private practice. I was afraid to take the National Counselor Examination because I thought I was going to fail. I was afraid if I failed, I wouldn't be able to get more money from my family to take the exam again. If I passed the exam, I was fearful of doing something wrong and getting arrested by the board of examiners in counseling. (By the way, they don't arrest you.) I was afraid that I would not document something correctly and I would be disqualified from practicing. I was afraid that a client would commit suicide on my watch. I was afraid I would not be able to make enough money to create a comfortable lifestyle for myself. I was afraid that if I went into private practice, no one would take advantage of my services because I lived in a small town of about 20,000 people and grew up in an area of about 2500. Most of the people in the area only knew me as "Mimi". Many of them were family members or friends. Several of them were friends of my parents or they were a part of our church. There was not a lot of room for me to be profitable and serve without major dual relationships and confidentiality concerns.

After completing graduate school, fear had me stuck for three entire years. Even though I was paralyzed by fear, my rent did not care about my fear. I had to make something happen. This is how I ended up teaching at a behavioral facility for children with special needs. It was horrible. I was depressed and grieving my unexperienced dream because I was outside of my purpose and I knew it. I knew that I wanted more. Not to mention the fact that 37K for a salary was not enough to compensate me for all of the times I was yelled at by a parent, bitten by a child, contracted strep throat, and my Lord, do not even get me started on all of the potty training accidents. I wanted to be able to experience more in life, and there was no way around the fear. I had to go through it. My mind was still not set on what I wanted because the fear was still bigger than my faith.

Here's what shifted me. One of my older brothers had a medical crisis. I went to visit him in ICU, sang to him, and prayed for him. This particular day, he looked at me and said, "Kid what are you doing? You gotta get out of here. You gotta get away from here. There's so much more for you out there." I hadn't told him about my career problem. It was a true God moment. He was right, but my heart was tied to my hometown and my family because it was all I ever knew. Leaving was beyond the depth of my comfort zone because I was home.

A few years prior when I was in high school, both of my parents passed away within about a year of each other. It shook me to my core. Seeing my brother fight for his life in the same hospital where my parents were, til this day makes my heart sink. A few days after my brother and I had that conversation, my brother passed away. At this point, I had a choice. I could either fight through fear, grief, anxiety, and trauma to relocate and pursue my dreams, or I could stay in my hometown and watch my dream of private practice also pass away along with those I loved. I chose to fight and leave. I needed a break from the constant grief triggers and reminders of an absent and dismantled immediate family. I knew that this plan had to work. There was not an option to move back in with my parents and save money until I figured out my next move. I chose to take the little bit of strength that I had to start a brand new life away from everything and everyone I've ever known to chase a dream. I chased it down and made a significant impact on the mental health industry one step at a time. I survived by sleeping on a friend's futon couch and eating a healthy diet of peanut butter and jelly sandwiches, rice, and Lays potato chips for several months until I got a job as an assessment counselor. Soon after I got the job, the transmission went out on my car. So I had to catch rides and figure it out. I was determined to not give up my dream of private practice because of a series of inconveniences and temporary discomfort.

I share my journey with you so that you understand how much I empathize with your fear. I know what it feels like to see glimpses of glory and not know the steps to get there in real life. This book is the framework that I used to go from being trapped in fear to being the go-to business coach and thought leader in the mental health industry. I mapped out all of the steps I followed so that you don't have to waste any more precious time researching and guessing whether or not the steps will work for you. My steps work. My life and career are living proof. The success path I have mapped out for you is incredibly valuable. It all started with having a healthy mindset.

Mindset

As a cognitive behavioral therapist it is only right that I begin this book by teaching you about reframes. I mean, I wouldn't be a good therapist if I didn't. So when it comes to beginning your private practice, one of the things you have to do before you start is get your mind together. For many therapists, when it comes to having the conversation about mindset, it becomes some fairy tale mythological experience that's an on-and-off switch. I want to tell you right now that it is not. It's nothing close to that. If you are going to be in the right mindset to build a private practice, that means you have to get your mindset and your intention set on the type of lifestyle that you want. You have to do that now before you turn the page. Before you go to any other parts of this book, you have to know right now what it is that you want to create. This is about you. There is not a strategy on the planet that I can teach you about business, marketing, sales, or leadership that will work if your mindset consists of limiting core beliefs.

Limiting core beliefs can come from different places. Sometimes our limiting core beliefs come from childhood experiences. Sometimes they come from being in poverty or being raised in survival mode. Sometimes limiting beliefs come from the people that you are around and the things they are saying to you. Sometimes our limiting beliefs come from feelings of pressure rooted in perfectionism. You may not know how to be anything other than successful and accomplished. But this private practice thing has somehow brought you to your knees and you ended up with this book in your hands. Sometimes our core beliefs about private practice become limited because we have self-sabotaging behaviors that reinforce what we're not doing. That may lead to self-fulfilling prophecies.

Here is a way to get around this. Allow me to insert some hope here because I know that I am all in your business. There is a way to do some really deep intensive strategic inner work. This is something a therapist may be able to help you with. If you don't have a therapist and you have not done any inner work, I highly recommend considering one. The unhealed part of you may be triggered and may be causing you to struggle with your self-confidence or how much you believe in yourself, and your ability to do hard things. I have included some resources in the back of the book to help you to develop a healthy mindset.

Private practice is a journey that may bring out the best and the worst in you at the same time. There will be moments where you feel like you are an absolute rock star and you are doing all the things well. There will be other moments where you question whether or not you even deserve to have a degree or a license. You will have some sessions with clients where you feel like you're in over your head and you're drowning. You may even start to experience vicarious trauma, and if you are full-time in your private practice you may have little support. This means you will need to create your own support system. Your support system will already need to be in place before you get started in private practice because those moments will come. At times building your practice will be hard and scary, but it will be an opportunity for you to grow as a clinician.

Let's go a little deeper into the mindset. If you picked up this book because you were looking for a quick way to make money with minimal effort, minimal accountability, minimal integrity, and minimal investment from you, this book will not give you that. This book will stretch you. It will give you several key components that you need to evaluate and consider before you go deeper into the journey of private practice.

Over the years I have seen business bring out the best in people. People who thought they didn't have what it takes to be successful in business, they made it happen. People who always said they were not good at marketing or technology, now have a strong online presence. The reality is you don't know what you are capable of until you are actually put in a position where you push beyond your comfort zone. You can do hard things. You can make hard decisions. Some of the hard decisions will place you in an ethical dilemma and some of the decisions will scare you. Do it scared. You can do it! I believe in you.

So right now from a mindset perspective, you have to decide what type of private practice business owner you will be. How will you handle your decision-making process when you're in private practice and no longer have a boss? No one will be looking, and you have no accountability other than yourself. There will be moments where your mindset changes and evolves.In your business, you will have to make tough decisions that keep your integrity in tact, protect your clients, and line up with the ethical standards of the mental health profession. The inner catacombs of your mind, your secret desires, and your truest intent for private practice will reveal the posture of your heart toward the people you serve. That my friends is really the core of what mindset is.

What things are YOUR mind set on? Is it living in a really safe neighborhood with good schools and a great community with easy access to amenities in your city? Are you set on being able to pay off your student loans? Are you set on being able to take a vacation and not worry about PTO getting approved? Are you set on being able to see only ideal clients that set your soul on fire every day? Are you set on creating wealth and a legacy for your family?

Roadmap

I have done my research. I know that many of you will pick up this book and read it in hopes of me revealing a secret checklist of how to start a private practice. Here's the thing, there are no secret tricks or checklists. The step-by-step things you need to know and do are on Google. The checklists all work for someone, but they may not work for you. ***If you have the checklist, and you've done all of the things, then why do YOU not have the thriving private practice that you desire?*** The words in this book are written to help you start to look inward and make the changes that need to be made to create a roadmap for your private practice. You need to create core values and beliefs for how you do business. You need a living, breathing document or standard operating procedures to guide you in your values, decision-making, events, marketing, and anything else you desire to do. This is your personal roadmap for your practice. Create your own document as you learn new things along your journey. The roadmap helps you remain focused when you get shiny object syndrome and want to do multiple things at once. Move in the season that you are in and slow down. Allow your roadmap to help you stay focused. I provide a full PDF roadmap for all of the students who are in my programs. It immediately helps with anxiety about building a private practice. You can also create your own, it doesn't have to be fancy. Take advantage of some of the bonus resources I have provided for you to help you create your own roadmap.Go to https://www.cbrewerconsulting.com/ceoclinicianbookbonus.

Good Habits in Private Practice

The determining factor of the success of your practice is the way you treat people, the way you show up every day and the story or reputation that follows you. I have been in the industry long enough to know that many therapists who choose the path of private practice are not genuinely in it to help people. They are genuinely in it to help themselves. Through my framework, I teach you how to genuinely care for your clients as well as yourself.

As a part of caring for yourself, you need good habits or self care. An example of a good habit could be going to bed around the same time every night and waking up around the same time every morning. You could also incorporate exercise into your daily routine. Making sure that you eat balanced meals, healthy snacks, and drink plenty of water are all good habits. Taking time to decompress after a long day of work is a good habit. Setting and enforcing boundaries around your client schedule and family time is a good habit. Creating designated days for coffee dates or networking meetings is a good habit. Scheduling weekends to unplug from all devices and enjoy nature is a good habit. Blocking off one weekend per quarter to get away and try something new is a good habit. Building a private practice around your personal life and not the other way around is a good habit.

I wanted to spend some time breaking down what good habits could possibly look like for you because at a certain point as a CEO clinician you are going to need mental and physical stamina to maintain the success you have created. It's hard to be creative and inspired when you are sleep deprived, nutrient deficient, and experiencing major burnout. So my recommendation is for you to go ahead and start implementing good habits now so you can be ready to operate at your highest self.

Learning Moment

Set your intentions every day. Start to develop good habits to take care of yourself so you can take care of your clients. Remember that self care is not selfish. It is a part of nurturing the greatest asset to your private practice which is you.

What good habits will you implement this week? Write them below.

____

____

____

____

____

CHAPTER 2:
THE ANXIOUS THERAPIST

Podcast Episode #116 Private Practice from an Anxious Perspective

To start off I want to share with you a little bit about my journey with anxiety and how it really showed up when I transitioned into private practice. Let's go back just a little bit so you will have context about why I decided to become a CEO clinician in the first place.

My childhood up to the age of 6 was very normal and beautiful, and then it turned chaotic. I have a very long history of sexual abuse by some of the adults who were supposed to be safe people. This abuse lasted from the time I was 6 years old to age 16 years old, and I never told my parents. I was raised in a military family who took protecting and serving to another level. I knew if I shared my experience that I had been violated, the integrity of my family system would never be the same. I chose to remain silent. I never went to therapy as a child or a teenager; it wasn't a thing. My parents were pastors, and no one in our immediate family, community, or extended neighborhood went to therapy.

I developed anxiety, rightfully so, and it just changed forms throughout different seasons of my life. My father became very ill when I was about 13. He struggled with his health for the next 4 years, and I watched him go in and out of hospitals. I watched my military hero's health decline dramatically during this time. My mother was there as a good wife right by his side, which meant I was at home alone being independent. I had to learn to be structured and disciplined . I had been cooking, cleaning, doing my laundry, doing my homework, getting ready for school, taking myself to school, leaving school to either go to work or go to practice since I can remember. I played every sport, and I made straight A's and an occasional B, but the anxiety was relentless. I don't remember really enjoying being a little girl after age 6.

I was a freshman in high school, anxious and still not in therapy. When I was a junior in high school, my father passed away. The following year right after graduation, we found out my mother was diagnosed with breast cancer. She passed away in the fall when I was 18 years old. Clinically at this point, I met the criteria for PTSD, complicated grief, generalized anxiety disorder, and several others.

I was an undergrad psychology student at Harding University. Soon after the spring semester, I started to really struggle emotionally. I did not have the words to even articulate everything I was feeling but I knew something was off. My mental health declined significantly. I stopped going to class. I lost my academic scholarship. I stopped eating. I had panic attacks all day long. If I was awake or if I was laying down, it did not matter. There was no peace. I hit rock bottom. I was completely hopeless and became suicidal. My anxiety was still through the roof at this point. I had to make a decision about whether or not I was going to work on myself, finish my psychology degree, become a therapist, and build a private practice. Remember there was no backup plan. There was no option to move back home, I had to figure it out. There was no option for me to go talk to my parents for wise counsel or to figure out what I should do. It was all or nothing and anxiety had to come with me.

Learning Moment

Here was the shift. I started talking to anxiety like a person."Dear anxiety, I don't need you. I am not afraid, but I am grieving. My heart is heavy, but I have an assignment to do. I have a psychology exam to prepare for. I have a research paper to do. My internship starts in a few weeks. Anxiety, you're welcome to come with me or you can stay here. It doesn't really matter to me, but I have something to do. People are going to need my services. I need to get prepared to serve them."

Now part of the reason I share that story with you is so you can have insight into the type of background that I have and why I'm so passionate about this work. I know that if my family knew a therapist who was black, Christian, shared our values, and was really skilled at what they did, they would have put me in therapy. It would have been the right thing to do and my family values supportive services. Even though they didn't know about the abuse, I know that if we had therapists who were present in our community being vocal about mental health, advocating about mental health disparities, advocating about insurance, treatment options, and medication options, I would have gotten help. If we would have seen an example of the therapist I described, someone would have put me in therapy. But, it never happened, and until this day I am recovering from the trauma AND working as a full-time CEO and private practice therapist.

Imposter Syndrome

"You are a therapist AND a business owner. You are not pretending to be one or the other." -Cameisha

I think it's only appropriate for us to have a conversation about imposter syndrome. I have mixed feelings about imposter syndrome, what it is, what it looks like, how it is presented to different people, and the behaviors associated with it. In my opinion, there is nothing about being a licensed clinician in the mental health field that would meet the criteria for a social label of imposter syndrome. Typically when we hear the term imposter syndrome it refers to or describes a person who is pretending to be someone they are not. People exhibiting characteristics of imposter syndrome often have to learn the traits, mannerisms, and personality of the subject they're pretending to be. This takes a lot of work, and regardless of how long it takes someone to attempt to embody all aspects of another person. At the end of the day, the lack of authenticity will become obvious.

Now if you're the type of clinician that I think you are reading this book, I already know that your mind has taken you down a path of a series of diagnoses to describe imposters and the pathological presentation of imposter syndrome. So let's connect this to the reality that there is no way for licensed mental health professionals to be imposters. In order to do what we do someone would have to EARN a bachelor's degree and a master's degree. We go through internship, and practicum, pass our boards, and we are under supervision for 3,000 hours. This means that it takes us at least 5 years to become who we are. There is no way to intentionally try to become someone we're not for 5 years. We literally evolve into a clinician day by day, case by case, hour by hour, treatment plan by treatment plan. There is no pretending. The work that we do if we are not careful can jeopardize our license, our clients, and the safety of our families. No one in their right mind would pretend to step into a field with that many risks.

So let's insert some truth. You are not pretending to be a licensed clinician, that is who you are. You are also not pretending to be a business owner. That is who you are becoming and for many of you, the first step on your journey was reading this book. All of these moving parts of who you are, what you do, who you're becoming, the life you're building, and the practice you're developing, is not an accident. This requires intentionality , grit, faith, stamina, and an unwavering belief that you have what it takes to build a private practice. So if you don't take anything else away from this chapter I want you to repeat this affirmation statement: ***I am a therapist AND a business owner. I am not an imposter.***

Now I know some may be thinking, this affirmation is cool, but what do I do about the anxiety I feel in the moment? When it's time for me to do the work I get really scared. I feel really anxious because I really don't know what I'm doing. You may be very anxious about building a private practice.

You have questions about whether or not you can do it, whether or not you have what it takes, and whether or not you can make enough money to pay your bills. Maybe you have thoughts about whether or not you should leave your agency, whether or not you should join a group practice, or go solo and be on your own. None of these options are wrong. Do whatever your heart desires and take the next best step for you. It doesn't matter if others disagree with your decisions for your life. People need your services. If you can focus on the pain, the trauma, the heartache, and the tears of your ideal client, you will say ***YES*** to the work that is required of you.

When you say yes you will show up and you will build the practice because you recognize that people need you. The only reason they're not getting what they need is because they don't know you exist. The reason they don't know you exist is that you haven't marketed to them and you haven't created a presence online and offline. I will teach you that in part 3. You are at a very pivotal point in your life. You need to decide whether or not you believe that the needs and mental health challenges of the people that you are called to serve are bigger than the amount of anxiety you feel about getting started. If this is true about you, keep reading.

CHAPTER 3:
DEVELOPING A BUSINESS MINDSET

Podcast Episode # 107 Developing a Business Mindset

As a business owner, you have to have a mindset that will essentially help you build success in your private practice now and as you scale in the future. To get started, the first thing you need to know about developing a business mindset is to have a plan of where you're going, what you want to accomplish, and by when. A lot of the therapists we serve have no roadmap for what they are building. In my company, we ask new therapists about their pain points. We ask about what's not working, and where they are stuck. We want to make sure that we are serving you and meeting your needs based on what you identified as a problem. One of the things I often hear is, "I don't know where to start." This is very common if you're a brand new therapist or if you are an established therapist who never developed a business mindset. You are not going to know where to start and that's okay. You need a big goal and a vision. Breaking things down into smaller goals will help you reach the big goal. ***In order to reach big goals you have to reach small goals first and the small goals***

have to be in alignment with sequential steps to get you to the BIG Goal. For example, how much money do you want to make and by what date? Do you have vacations planned? Do you have a special project on the horizon like buying a home? Do you have a teenager who's a sophomore in high school and you know within the next two years you need to fund their college experience?

When just starting out, you need to be strategic with the limited amount of time you have and the limited amount of money you have. Life is way too expensive for experiments in private practice. As a business owner with a business owner mindset, you need to invest in high-quality services, training, coaching, and mentorship that will help you do whatever you want to do.

Beyond this point, the decisions you make are not personal, they are business decisions. You will have clients who don't show up for a session and you need to enforce your policy and charge them a late fee. It's not personal, it's business. At a certain point as a therapist, you will no longer be able to do a speaking engagement for anything less than 500.00 even if it is for a church or a non-profit. It's not personal, it's business. There will be software systems you need to invest in to streamline the entire operations of your practice. Some of these software systems are not cheap, so don't complain. It's not personal, it's business. You may have a friend who is a photographer who wants to do a photoshoot for you, but they are not that good. It's okay to hire someone else who is more experienced. It's not personal, it's business. Removing your heart from the business decisions that you need to make will help you learn how to make decisions faster for the sake of your private practice. This is why you need a business mindset and not just a personal mindset about business.

Comparison

One of the most damaging things you could do in private practice to slow down your progress is to engage in comparison. Comparison literally takes your eyes off of what you're doing, who you're serving, and what you're building and allows them to wander over to someone else's practice. You will begin to judge yourself through the lens of what you are only allowed to see in someone else's practice. What makes this so dangerous is that many times therapists start making changes and adjustments to their own practice without having a full understanding of why someone else is doing what they're doing. The decisions I currently make at this stage of my private practice will not make sense to someone who is six months in. I now make decisions based on the data, revenue, my goals, my team, and where I am in my personal life. For a therapist just starting out with no revenue, no data, no team, no projects, no partnerships, and no collaborations, there is no reason you and I need to make business decisions in the same way. Does that mean my practice is better than yours? Absolutely not. It means my practice is different and I've been doing this for longer than you which means there is nothing for you to change. There is nothing for me to change. What is true is that we each need to honor the stage of private practice that we're in, do it well, and evolve. The evolution of your practice and the acceptance of that evolution will keep you anchored. It will keep you grounded and it will build your confidence and your ability to navigate your practice.

There have been times when people who worked outside of my company found me online and were bold enough to send me an email about the things I needed to do differently in my business, and TOLD me to report back to them after I had made the changes. Whatever feelings came up for you in your body while reading that sentence were the same ones I had times 87. That may have been an opportunity for me to start considering their recommendations and make very impulsive decisions and changes in my practice. But I had to remember that the person making the recommendation was an outsider. They do not know me, my vision, or the direction of my life. Therefore that disqualifies them. One thing I want you to take away from this chapter about comparison is ***that you are the expert in your private practice.*** I understand that you're new. I understand that you're learning. I understand you may not be new, but you still may not have the success you desire. Always remember that you are the CEO of your private practice. Anyone you choose to work with, to hire, to go to for mentoring or coaching has to submit to your leadership because you are the vision carrier. Even if you choose me as your coach at the end of this book I will ask you, "CEO what would you like to do? What decision would you like to make?"

Learning Moment

So here is your takeaway from this chapter: do not allow unsolicited, unqualified people to provoke you to make changes in your private practice when you are the vision carrier for your practice. Guard your ideas. Guard your vision and make decisions that will move you forward *EVERY DAY*.

Incorporating Rest

I'm all about forward movement, making improvements, progressing, and refining. But from a business mindset standpoint, there are times and seasons within private practice I think you should do nothing. And for those who have high-functioning anxiety and are always busy, I know you're triggered, but stay with me. The reason there are seasons where you should do nothing is that you have to be able to enjoy the fruits of your labor in the current season at some point. If you worked hard to get your first five clients, be still. Spend a few weeks or a few months just serving your five, because when five goes to 10 things change. You'll never be the same. So whatever stage you're in, sit there, dwell in it, bask in it, savor every moment. Every phase of your private practice going forward will either be a dream, a nightmare, or a combination of both. So when it's comfortable, enjoy it. When it's not enjoyable, try to enjoy it anyway. The difficult seasons are the seasons that reveal your leadership. They reveal your business mindset. They reveal your business decision-making skills, and if you struggle consistently to make $1,000 per month, you will drown making $5,000 per month. Be careful what you wish for if you're not willing to work for it. A part of working for it is working to keep it, which means retention and keeping clients on your caseload.

Retention & Rejection

As a business owner with a business owner mindset, it is very easy to take this personally when a client stops services with you for whatever reason. In my experience, when clients are choosing a therapist they are looking for specialized help. They are looking for someone who has experience treating the EXACT thing they are struggling with. Even though you are trauma-informed or trauma-certified, you are not an expert in all traumas. If you start seeing a client and they soon realize that you are not the best fit for the struggle they are experiencing, they may stop services. Try not to panic. Reach out, check on them, make sure they are safe, do a safety plan, make a referral, and document everything. After that, try not to internalize them advocating for themselves as if there is something wrong with you as a person. You may be a wonderful therapist, however, if you cannot help them or they don't feel connected to you, people have every right to move on. When you are first starting, you may feel triggered or rejected. Someone's decision to move on is personal FOR THEM. It doesn't have to be personal for you as the business owner. Allow clients to flow and advocate for themselves. A great way to decrease the likelihood of clients flowing in and out of your practice is through clear strategic marketing and fostering a great customer service experience. When you are clear it helps you to attract ideal clients who you can help.

New business mindset affirmation statement: ***Clients deserve to choose the therapist who is the best fit for their needs. I deserve to work with ideal clients who are a part of my scope of work and my statement of intent that I can confidently serve. Their decisions are personal. My decisions are business.***

PART 2

MONEY OF A CEO CLINICIAN

CHAPTER 4:
COMPENSATION MADE EASY

"The hardest part about getting compensated as a therapist is believing that your service is valuable enough to be compensated appropriately. The challenge is to do it without trying to make people pay you your worth and get your validation from within." -Cameisha

Podcast Episode # 108 Principle of Cash Flow

This is the part of the book where things start to go to another level. In this chapter, I will be teaching you how to be compensated for your services with ease. The reason I say with ease is if you follow the steps, apply the strategy I teach you, and show up in a way so people don't have to question whether or not you're the therapist for them, they will pay you.

A part of my work as a thought leader in the mental health industry, specifically in the realm of business and mindset, is to challenge the myths and misconceptions of the industry and speak the truth as needed. This is a place where truth is needed, so here is the truth. The belief that people should pay you your worth is not how business works. Your worth as a service provider is determined by the value and the results that you can clearly articulate to a potential client. If a potential client does not confidently believe that you possess the clinical skills, training, and expertise that is needed to help them meet their treatment goals, they will not pay you. Your potential clients do not care about your personal beliefs regarding your own worth. They want to know if you can help them. They also want to know if you can get them there in the shortest time frame possible. This is true whether you consider yourself to be a solution-focused therapist or not.

In today's society, prospective clients are not interested in working with someone for years upfront. Now many clients do stay in treatment long-term, however, some of the long-term treatment is for the presenting issues and not the initial challenges that were present during the intake. People stay in treatment because life continues to happen and they want to continue to work with the same provider. Many people also stay in treatment if the services have been helpful. This is called retention. If the services have not been helpful for them in their first few sessions, they have no incentive to stay longer. Therefore, your first session needs to be about building rapport, but it also needs to be about productivity. Productivity is measured by the client. Based on my experience, many clients will be coming to therapy treatment for the first time and they expect to see change and progress in their presenting symptoms quickly. You should validate their urgency and help them set realistic expectations around what the therapeutic relationship looks like.

Learning Moment
Integrity Pause: Please do not intentionally move slowly through the treatment process because you want to continue seeing someone for as long as possible. Strengthen your marketing plan for continuous referrals and help your clients get what they came for so both of you can move forward.

Now that we have that understanding and you are clear on charging your worth and understanding that people pay for the value that you can articulate based on what they deem is worthy, we can talk about how to make compensation easy for you. What problems can you help them with and how are you going to help them? If you can get really clear on what their problems are, what your solution is, and how you will support them in the process, it will decrease the time of a lengthy decision-making period that buyers often go through. I know that even using the term buyer to describe prospective therapy clients may make you cringe, but remember this book is about business, this is not personal. Yes, we need to see them as human beings, but at this point, we're not talking about building rapport, we're talking about the exchange and the transaction for services. If you don't get an understanding of how you're going to approach the transactional component that happens before they actually become a client of yours, they will never become a client of yours.

Strategy for Compensation

So let's talk about the strategy on how to get you paid. The way I teach this as a part of the CEO Clinician framework is that the key to your compensation is in your "I help" statement. The key is in you being clear about what you offer and who you serve. You need to make sure that you are not being a generalist. I teach therapists how to niche down when they're just starting out, and then as your practice grows, you can expand your target market.

Here's an example of an "I help" statement: I help newly divorced men overcome anxiety, shame, and fear, and learn to move forward with their lives. Another example is, I help college students learn to confidently develop a social life, manage their stress, and achieve their academic goals. Having these types of really clear statements as a part of your initial marketing plan will help you understand where you need to go and where you need to position yourself to meet the type of clients you desire to serve.

For those of you who want to go deeper in my courses and coaching programs, I will give you scripts of what to say, how to say it, and how to continue the conversation. The goal is to go where your clients spend time so you can stop waiting for them to find you. If you follow my strategy, you will have access to these very specific types of prospective clients for years to come. If prospective clients are not clear on who you serve, and how you help them, they won't want to work with you. You need to make it easy for people to make a decision. Make it easy for people who are probably in crisis when they start researching therapists in their area who accept their insurance or only accept cash. Make it easy for them to make a decision to hire you. Believe it or not, the key to your compensation isn't really in all the fancy bells and whistles. It is the statement that sets you apart from the thousands of other therapists online or offline. It is the statement that helps people make a decision and it helps you be compensated. It can be easy if you let it be. My encouragement to you is to let it be easy.

Let's be practical. I'm going to give you a homework activity. I want you to take the next few lines that I've provided and write out your I-help statement. You are not married to it. It's not forever, it's for now. When you try to attract everyone, you attract no one. This statement is to get you started for now, or it's for your next level if you're ready to scale your practice. Who will you serve? What problems are you helping them solve? How will you serve them?

(I help______experiencing__________related to ____to learn to __________)

Make sure you register for the next 3-day challenge or workshop so I can coach you through this if you need help.

https://www.cbrewerconsulting.com/3daychallenge

____

____

____

____

____

____

____

____

COMPENSATION MADE EASY CHAPTER RECAP

- Charge rates that help you meet your goals for your family and your practice.
- Gain your validation and self-worth from within, not from what others think.
- Become the expert in your area of expertise through learning and honing your skills.
- Create an "I help" statement that clearly communicates who you help and how.
- Learn to clearly and concisely articulate the results that you help people accomplish.
- Document your journey and share your personal success and testimonials of those you have helped.

CHAPTER 5:
SYSTEMS & TECHNOLOGY

"You can either be a boomer and hate technology or you can take advantage of the blessing of automation to make your life easier through technology."

Podcast Episode #112 What it Takes to Run a Private Practice

Did you know that I am technologically challenged ? My team believes that I am tech savvy, knowledgeable, innovative, and all the things. No matter what I tell them, they believe something different about me than what I believe about myself. So indulge me for a moment, and I'll tell you how my relationship with technology started. At the peak of the pandemic in 2020, I was working for an agency when things shifted immediately. We needed to create ways to provide treatment and therapy to patients even if they were sick or showing symptoms of said virus.

When I got my first taste of doing virtual group therapy, it changed the way I approached mental health treatment completely. It created a hunger and a curiosity to learn more about the creative and innovative ways to use technology and other systems to reach people who needed treatment. I started working with a coach and business mentor who taught me about different software systems where I could provide online coaching, online courses, online workshops, master classes, etc. Because I knew that I had built a presence offline in my area, my next step was to build a presence online. Here's what changed everything for me. ***Having clear marketing strategies in place about how to approach each of my platforms, I knew that I had created the perfect recipe for unlimited income.*** I can literally create a digital product in the next hour, add a price tag, and send out an email and generate sales TODAY.

Because of what I have done over the years, I see the value in upgrading my tech systems. I upgraded the types of software for my consulting practice and my therapy practice. The systems for my therapy practice require different things than my coaching systems.

Every aspect of your business doesn't need to be HIPAA compliant. Please relax. Some therapists are so concerned about confidentiality to the point that they are not profitable in business. Everything is not a secret. You do not work for the secret service. If your services are secret, you won't be compensated for what you do. People have to know who you are in order to pay you. Use technology and systems to help you get your services to the people who need them.

For the sake of education, you need to know that in the online space when someone refers to you having a system, that could mean several things. A system may not be technology-based at all. A system may be the step-by-step process you have implemented to execute a certain task. A system can be your processes, your procedures, or the sequence of events that you go through when you're onboarding a new client. Onboarding means when they start working with you. You're probably already implementing a system and you're not aware. Do you call them? Do you email them your informed consent form? Do they upload a copy of their driver's license and insurance card? Do they enter their credit card information and save it so you can run their payment after each session? How do they contact you between appointments? How do they reschedule their appointment should something come up? All of this is a part of onboarding.

If you automate all of those steps and you use a computer, an app, or some type of online tool, you're implementing technology into the system. I'm telling you this because sometimes what I see in the industry is therapists hating technology because they believe that in order to have a system, they have to use technology. That is not true. The goal should be to optimize or automate the system. This will make the system more streamlined so that you don't have to be a part of every moving step. When you automate all of your steps in the system for a particular task that takes a prospective client from one point all the way to an endpoint, that's called a funnel. For those of you who are visual learners, like me, please do not stress or worry. I have videos, courses, and coaching programs to show you visually and in a very colorful way what this looks like. If you are going to be in private practice, group practice, or solo practice, you have to develop a healthy relationship with both systems and technology. You cannot have one without the other because your systems are what makes the technology work.

Technology is becoming more advanced with artificial intelligence and things like Chat GPT. If you are an old-school therapist, you can hate it and resist evolution all day long, but it's not going to matter. Technology will continue to evolve. You can try to keep up, try to learn, try to customize it, and integrate it into what you do, or you can soon have an outdated practice. It's totally up to you. I've seen therapists do both. In my opinion, one of the saddest things I've ever seen is very talented clinicians struggling to fill their caseload, but they also have a deep-rooted sense of hatred toward all of the advanced systems and technology that can make a huge difference in their practice.

Learning Moment

What I want you to take away from this chapter is that technology cannot replace the power of human connection. You are uniquely positioned to bring your brilliance into your practice and use technology to get it out into the world. In order to do this, you have to believe that you have what it takes to add technological tools to your business, but not to replace your therapeutic skill set. You are not a robot. You are irreplaceable. People may try to take your place and say therapists are not needed. To me, that sounds like an opportunity for mental health professionals to advocate and educate the masses about our power and purpose. There's a space for you, the reader of this book, but you have to be big enough and bold enough to take up that space and to be seen and heard. Use technology to amplify the power of who you are and how you advocate for people who need mental health treatment. Use technology to shed light on mental health disparities and create opportunities for people to get access to care. Use technology to take stress off of your plate, so you can do what you do well. Use technology to build the type of business that supports your lifestyle and helps you take care of your family. Become a sponge in the world of technological advancement and mental health.

There may be venture capitalists looking for opportunities to buy your practices. Don't let them bully you. Now if you want to sell your practice, we cover that in my advanced-level group coaching program. That's a great way to pivot in your career or retire with some major cash. Please remember tech startups and venture capitalists will continue to build companies to mimic shortened versions of mental health care. It will happen faster if we sit back and do nothing. I still believe in the mental health field. I still believe that we have one of the most incredible careers on the planet. I'm not oblivious to the pace of the economy and the volatility of insurance companies and pharmaceutical companies. I'm very much aware, but I choose to stay focused on the joys and the power of technology and how many people we can help if we use technology to our advantage.

I hope that your heart is stirred and provoked. I hope you have taken some time to examine your own thoughts and reservations about technology and how it applies to you. I hope you're already deciding that you're going to stop saying things like, "I'm not good at technology," "I hate computers," or "I don't know how to do that stuff." The only thing that's going to help you know how to do it is to learn how to do it. So for your action steps for this chapter, I would like for you to think about what technology systems you want to explore for your private practice and start viewing the systems as assets and not scary technology monsters. I can't wait to hear about what you create and how you stopped the mental technology monsters from stealing your dream.

Systems and Technology Chapter Recap

- Create clear marketing strategies for how you approach each platform.
- Remember you don't have to market on every platform.
- Go where your ideal clients are and make it easy for them to connect with you.
- Be visible in the areas where your ideal clients hang out.
- Embrace technology so that you can stop being hands-on in every part of your practice.
- Choose one technology platform and spend 30 minutes per day learning the features.
- Create standard operating procedures for how you run your business. (Yes this can be done in a Google doc. It doesn't have to be complicated.)
- Let it be easy, but let it be efficient.

CHAPTER 6:
PRICING & SALES

"Getting good at sales is not optional, it is a prerequisite for maintaining and scaling a private practice."
-Cameisha

Podcast Episode #109 Insurance vs. Private Pay

If you're going to be successful in private practice and operate as a CEO clinician you have to price your services in a way that makes sense for the people who are paying you and get good at selling to them. As much as we would like for everyone to be full-time private pay, it's not going to happen with 20+ clients who attend weekly sessions. As much as we would like for everyone to make $250 per hour for therapy, that is not real life. Even if you live in an area where that is the norm, if you're not very good at articulating who you are, what you do, and how your services are worth $250 an hour, people are not going to pay for it. This is especially true if they have the option to use their insurance and pay a $25 copay to a therapist down the street. Set your therapy sessions between $100-200 per hour. Make sure it's enough for you to pay the bills at home, for your business and to have some money left over for taxes or emergencies.

Business Trivia Question: What's the largest business expense you will ever have?

Answer: Taxes

Pause here to check out podcast episode #109 of the CEO Clinician Podcast. You can check it out at https://www.cbrewerconsulting.com/podcasts/the-ceo-clinician-podcast . After listening to the episode I hope you get a more realistic understanding and picture of setting your rates. Also, in Module 2 of my coaching program Private Practice Ready, I teach you the full budget breakdown of how to calculate how much you need for your home and how much you need to operate your practice. If you are going to be a CEO, you have to be the CEO of your home and of your business. So yes, this means two budgets! You need to account for every dollar that comes in and out of both entities.

Speaking Engagements

When it comes to setting your prices for expansion, there are several ways you can scale your practice. The quickest way in my opinion is through speaking engagements.

Speaking engagements can consist of workshops, trainings, presentations, virtual masterclasses, webinars, panel discussions, and podcasts. Any place where you have an opportunity to use your voice, provide education, and add value to an event or an audience is great for sales. You can be compensated for your talks whenever you get ready. In order to set your fees for doing speaking engagements as a new therapist, I recommend you start wherever you're comfortable. If you've never done a presentation, you've never done any speaking, and you're doing a 30 - 45 minute presentation, you can absolutely start off at $500. Now through coaching, I will support you in positioning yourself to make sure you show up in a way where people are ready to pay you $500 without questioning your rate.

As you get better at speaking, you will get more testimonials. You get more opportunities if you have a portfolio of you speaking at different types of events. You will be able to raise your prices, and your new norm can then become $1,500 minimum for you to speak. It happens every day. There are speakers in the industry who make $5,000 or more per talk, and they have the same degrees and licensure as you do. It can be done, however, there is a rite of passage to getting people to hire you for paid opportunities. From an integrity standpoint, I recommend that if you desire to make $1,000, you need to make sure you have invested $1,000 in someone else. Maybe you'll pay $1,000 for training, a conference, a course, or for a coaching program. I definitely think you need to know what it feels like to spend the same amount or more that you would like to be paid. There are a lot of therapists who desire to make $1,500 on one speaking engagement, but they are not willing to spend $250 on anything except a continuing education credit. There is a reason why it is so important to invest in the level that you want to earn because there are different rules. There's a different set of social norms, language, types of people, and a completely different atmosphere at different stages of investment.

This is the downfall of the business side of what we do. Other industries understand this principle. Based on my experience in the mental health industry, we are still lacking because we value training for EMDR more than we value coaching programs or intensives that help us learn the business skills and the strategy to make the money we need to take care of our families for years to come. You can have all the credentials in the world and still live paycheck to paycheck. You don't have to live one step above poverty simply because you are not good at generating sales or creating income. The level of clinical training doesn't equal income - mind-blown sorry.

I'm going to give you a quick homework activity. Please take a picture of it after you have completed it and DM me to let me know that it's done. I want you to write out your rates for the following:

What is your rate for a full intake therapy session?_________

What is your rate for individual sessions? _______________

What is your rate for a couple sessions or family sessions if you do these? ______________________________________

What is your sliding scale rate? ______________________

What are you willing to slide to?_________________________

What is your rate for speaking engagements ____________

Panels__________________

Keynotes________________

Workshops______________

A quick tip: Panel discussions tend to be free or much cheaper than what you would charge to do a keynote or a full workshop presentation where you're the only trainer and you're speaking for 30 to 45 minutes.

Here's another quick tip. Many of you might desire to book speaking engagements where you make $25,000 per contract. If you want to book large ticket speaking opportunities, you will mainly have to pitch to corporations or sell to universities that have budgets for those types of events and that is their norm for paying speakers. Typically it will be $25,000.00 over a period of time and you might bring your signature program to their campus or company and teach it 3-4 times per year. This is a contracted long-term project. If you're not ready for that, then you would sell locally to different types of businesses with different budgets which requires a different sales process.

So if you decide at this moment that you want a speaking coach, ask them if they teach therapists how to get booked by corporations or do they teach therapists how to get booked by other businesses, schools, colleges, nonprofits, churches, etc. It is a completely different strategy. I don't want you to be misled because there are speaking coaches who don't have integrity and will pitch you a dream that everybody can get booked to speak at the next Coca-Cola convention for $25,000 and that's not how that works. You can do it, but it is going to require something different of you and if you're not ready, that is okay. Just start somewhere.

The beginning of your marketing process for sales

Now that we have spent some time discussing pricing, let's talk more about sales and creating a process as a new therapist. There is a term to describe where people go from not knowing who you are, to learning about you, to reaching out to book a call, to getting on the consultation with you, to being accepted for services, to scheduling the first appointment, to filling out their intake forms and then having their first appointment. It is called a sales process, or in the digital marketing space, it is also called a funnel. In the Private Practice Ready Coaching Program, I'll take you deeper into what funnels look like and I'll teach you how to create your funnel. We will test your funnel repeatedly to make sure you have an active and working funnel because people can fall out of your funnel if there is anything wrong with the process that gets them from not knowing who you are to becoming a paid client.

You will do this process repeatedly to build your entire caseload. Once your caseload is filled, you will have to learn a new sales process to get other opportunities. If you decide to write a book and sell it, you need a sales process. This includes software, landing pages, email sequences, and a lot of other things. If you decide to create an online course, you will need a sales process again, software, landing pages, and an event to launch your course to the world. If you decide to do speaking engagements, you will need a sales process all the way through the pitch, proposal, negotiation of the contract, signing of the contract, and the consultation meeting. It may even be helpful to get attorneys involved. That is all a sales process.

In my experience, the reason people do not make money in their private practice and in scaling their private practice is simply because they are not good at sales, don't have a sales process, don't have funnels in place that work, and there's not enough people who know you exist. When you are first starting out in private practice, it's not enough to just have a directory profile with your information and make one post per month on social media. The market is not saturated, but it is noisy. There are a lot of people who are less qualified than you, have less experience than you, and have zero credentials or certifications, but they're making way more money than you. It's only because they created a product or service that people want, they learned how to market well, and they have a sales process that works. My mission as the author of this book and future coach for many of you reading the book is to help you position yourself in the industry and in the marketplace where you can shine. You deserve to make an impact because you're overqualified and you care about people for real. I'm not okay with therapists who have come in contact with me at any touchpoint being overqualified and underpaid. I can't make you be paid, but I can teach you how to get paid. It's up to you what you do with what you have learned through the teaching avenues I have made available to you. You have access to The CEO Clinician podcast, my live videos, the 3-day challenge, my email newsletters, my trainings, my webinars, my courses, and my coaching programs. Those are all of the touch points where I help therapists make an income and take care of the families. I can't do anything for you other than provide education and support you as you're implementing the curriculum from my framework. All of the touchpoints are part of the sales process. The book that's in your hands at this moment is a great first touch point to introduce you to who I am, what I do, the problems I solve, and how I help people.

Everything you do is a part of your sales process. So yes, you need to consistently show up on social media. Yes, you need to consistently show up in your community. Yes, you need to go to networking events related to your niche and be visible. Yes, you need to go to events that are not just for therapists. All those things are part of your sales process and marketing plan. If you're showing up and you have a visibility plan for online and offline, you're networking, you have your services packaged and priced, and you have things in place for people to contact you, and you have the back end of your business set up to do business, then sales will be easier for you. If you do not have these things done, you may become frustrated. You may lose money and you may be wasting time. You may even be there at this moment. Please don't fret, I'm here to support you. Pause here to take a deep breath, give yourself grace, and then keep reading.

Launching Coaching Services & Online Courses

The digital marketing landscape has changed since the pandemic. There was a different sense of urgency. People were investing in coaching programs and online courses like crazy. Some because they were desperate. For some, it was because they had lost their jobs. For some, it was simply because they were bored. People were buying $500 online courses on how to knit sweaters for their cats. The course creators were selling courses by the thousands; They were making 30 - 50 thousand dollars on online courses teaching you how to knit sweaters for a cat. Over the last couple of years, people still believe that they can create premium-price courses that solve entry-level problems with shallow content and expect to make the same type of money. That is no longer true. The industry has changed. The market has shifted. People have returned back to work. There are not as many people working from home. Travel has opened back up. People are taking longer to make buying decisions. People are taking their time to do research before they spend their money on courses, coaching programs, events, training, webinars, etc. People aren't as desperate for fluff anymore. They want real transformation and strategy that drastically changes their lives. There are sophisticated buyers who are not impulsive. You can serve them and help them accomplish their goals.

Learning Moment

This means you have to have a strategy for how you are going to navigate the post-pandemic space and set more realistic revenue goals for your business and your family.

This is also a Divine opportunity for the people who put together high-quality programs and content in any format to be able to get major attention. The people who are interested in depth and value will be attracted to who you are, what you do, and how you help people. They will be attracted to your therapy services. They will be attracted to your speaking engagements. They will want to bring you into their companies, organizations, and schools to serve their audience. This is the time for mental health professionals to show who the real credential carriers are. Not that we're in competition with the 30-minute pop-up life coaches, but some of the life coaches have gotten really bold and have attempted to do therapy with minimal training. As long as qualified people with master's degrees, thousands of hours of clinical training, additional hours of continuing education, sit on the sidelines because of fear and imposter syndrome, and insecurity, the 30 minute pop-up life coaches have no choice but to continue to go forth.

The space is unoccupied because therapists like you are leaving money on the table because you are waiting for the perfect time and you're not making sales. Now hear me, this is not a chapter about licensed therapists versus life coaches. This is still a chapter about sales and pricing. The life coaches of the world are not afraid to generate sales. They're not afraid to set their prices confidently and show up. People are looking for them. I honestly think there is a place for life coaches. I have made several referrals to life coaches for aftercare. After a client has met treatment goals and just wants to follow up with someone for accountability, a life coach is a great next step. When people no longer meet the criteria for medical necessity, it is time to refer out if you are billing insurance. Working alongside life coaches in the field is a really cool opportunity. However, there is a difference in treatment in what we do as licensed mental health professionals and what life coaches do. Don't ever forget that.

When it comes to pricing, generating sales, setting your rates, and adding value to the industry, you have to set realistic numbers for what can happen to you. It doesn't matter what you've seen other people make online. If you don't have sales systems in place, you may need to adjust the vision. Once you've met that goal for that phase of your practice, then we can go to the next level and expand.

Last tip before we close out. You need to get a jump start on your numbers if you're going to be good at sales. So if you know right now that you desire to be in private practice in the next 3 to 6 months, that means you need to start aggressively saving your money. You need to save for a rainy day for your household and your business. You need to work really hard to start building your caseload because you need to save that money for emergencies for your private practice. You need to save money for your taxes. Those quarterly tax payments are coming no matter what. You are going to have to pay them. However, in order to get out of this negative cycle of living paycheck to paycheck in your private practice, you have to create your own overflow. You can do it by appropriately pricing a product/service people really want and selling to them consistently. For you as a new therapist that means you need to have vision and be looking ahead for what events you want to do when you launch your practice. How many therapy clients do you want to have before you publicly announce your launch? I teach you how to launch your practice through my coaching programs, because making a post on social media is not a launch. If you have it positioned right, you have services priced right and you have enough therapy clients or speaking engagements already on the books, you can relax. ***The goal is to feel good about your practice and have a steady stream of referrals.*** I teach the students in my programs a strategy that is a repeatable process. I don't teach you things that are trendy, because trends fade. I teach you solid foundational systems of marketing, business strategy, and business operations and leadership that have stood the test of time. The goal is for your practice and the income you've made to last and serve you well into your retirement years.

Pricing & Sales Chapter Recap

- "Getting good at sales is not optional. It is a prerequisite for maintaining and scaling a private practice"-Cameisha
- Your pricing strategy needs to also include how much you need for expenses, taxes & profit.
- Set realistic revenue goals so you don't get overwhelmed.

- ***The goal is to feel good about your practice and have a steady stream of referrals.***
- ***You need a simple sale strategy that's a repeatable process so you can have predictable income.***
- Your practice and the income you've made can last and serve you well into your retirement years if you set it up that way.
- Show up online and offline! To generate sales, you need to be found doing what it is that you say you do. If you serve single moms, then go to events for single moms.
- Invest in business coaching and sales training to learn a custom strategy to really start to generate income in your practice without the headache.

PART 3

MARKETING OF A CEO CLINICIAN

CHAPTER 7:
RELATIONSHIP-BASED MARKETING

Podcast Episode #101 Why New Therapists Should be Marketing

Relationship-based marketing is the most effective strategy for therapists to build a private practice. I do not care how much people try to convince you to believe that getting to know people well and establishing a relationship with them is not the best method for building your private practice. Later in the next chapter, I will teach you about how to create a presence online and offline because you do need both.

Before we begin, we need to start with your mindset around marketing. If you have made it to this portion of the book, this is not the time to start playing small. This is also not the time to rekindle old patterns of thinking about your ability to market your private practice. One of the most strategic things I have ever taught therapists about business is how to get to know people who can send them referrals. Marketing is a long game. The way you market yourself today will determine the type of income you make in the future. Your ability to be strategically found by the people who are looking for your services will greatly contribute to the type of lifestyle you can afford for your family. In the industry, when you hear people talking about positioning and visibility, all that means is you are no longer operating as a best-kept secret. This means you are actively seeking out and cultivating relationships with people so that you and your practice are always top of mind when they hear about a prospective client for you. Please make sure you put this part in your notes as well. It is your responsibility to market your private practice. I do not recommend that you leave the success and longevity of your practice in the hands of a website, SEO, social media online directories, and paid ads.

The reason for this is that you don't have control over any online platform or tool. Therefore, if the internet shuts down or the platforms you have been using to market go away and you do not have any other marketing strategies that don't require you to be online, you and your practice are in trouble. I have been a business coach for entrepreneurs for several years and what I have discovered is that there is a gripping belief that if you make a few posts on social media and share a few videos, then that will guarantee that your private practice will be full. I need you to understand that this is not true, and it takes more to market a private practice than most people think. My position as the author of this book is to help you reframe your beliefs, take you behind the scenes, and help you create your path in the mental health industry.

Learning Moment - Good solid strategic relationships will get you farther than good online marketing ever will.

Now please understand I am not opposed to using online marketing strategies. Several of the online marketing strategies that I have used over the years have significantly impacted our ability to reach people and increase our visibility. But I also know that online marketing is only one part of an overall marketing strategy. So I teach therapists how to build an online presence as well as an offline presence.

Relationship Based Marketing Chapter Recap

- Marketing is a long game so be patient as you are creating your marketing strategy.
- Good solid strategic relationships will get you farther than good online marketing ever will.
- Take time to go on coffee dates to get to know other business owners.

- Diversify your relationships beyond networking with other therapists. Go meet people in other industries who also serve the people in your niche.
- Two to three times per week post about your practice and how people can work with you.
- Once per month text everyone on your contact list, send them information about your practice, and tell them you are accepting new clients. Ask them to copy and paste and share it with their contacts and on their social media pages.

CHAPTER 8:
CREATING A PRESENCE

Podcast Episode #119 Being Relevant as a Therapist

Developing your online presence as a therapist consists of 3 parts: content creation, engagement, and strategy. Allow me to add a brief disclaimer. I am not a social media expert. I do not have any formal education in marketing. However, I know what works for therapists because that's who I serve every day. Let's break this down.

Tips for content creation:

- Create posts that add value to other people's lives. These posts can be educational, informational, or for entertainment.
- Don't just reshare quotes and graphics from other practices or other mental health clinics. Be creative and allow your zone of genius to show.

Tips for engagement:

- Build a relationship online by commenting on others' posts, asking questions, and replying to comments on your posts.

- Do live-stream videos with others.
- Be friendly and soon people will go to your page to learn more about who you are and what you do.
- Make sure your links, content, and information are easy for others to find.

Be intentional about how you navigate the online space. There are seasons in private practice where your focus may be to just increase the number of people who are following your page. In other seasons, you may focus on strengthening your online relationships for future collaborations. In some seasons you may use your online presence to drive traffic to your services which will increase sales of your products and services. All of these things require a different strategy and a different mindset. Allow me to add a hard truth statement. If you are using the wrong strategy at the wrong time, you may not get the results you are looking for.

Lights, Camera, Action

This is the part of the chapter where you may get really camera shy, but try to fight it. This is also the chapter where you move beyond your temporary discomfort. Social media and other online platforms are incredible ways to increase your caseload. You need to know the exact platform where your ideal clients hang out and where they would go to find mental health services. This may be two different places. You also need to know that what you are posting is resonating with the clients who would be interested in your services. The question becomes, how do I know if my content resonates with my target audience? Answer - you ask them. This is called market research. One of the ways I see a lot of therapists waste time and get frustrated with their online presence is by committing to creating content and posting daily with ZERO understanding of whether or not the content is what their target audience is interested in. You need to know the top 10-20 questions or problems your ideal clients are facing. We are long past the days of half showing up, doing the bare minimum, and expecting to make 5k-10k+ per month.

Learning Moment

You may view yourself as amazing, but if you are marketing to a group of people who do not see the value in your services because you have not properly marketed to them, they will not buy your services.

If you choose to play it safe regarding your online marketing presence by just doing content creation, engagement, or strategy you will not be able to maximize your marketing. If this all sounds overwhelming, just remember you don't have to do this alone. You can decide to work with me and my team so we can support you through it and help you build the online side of your business.

Now if you are one of those people who just prefers the offline space, this portion of the book is for you. You can build your private practice entirely offline. Your marketing strategy will depend on who your ideal clients are. The bottom line is you need to network at the events where your ideal clients would be or where decision-makers who have access to your ideal clients would be. Also, if you prefer in-person events, take advantage of your local chamber of commerce. This is where the decision-makers in your city hang out. Get to know them. Learn about what they do. Share about your practice as well as your other skill sets. Be clear and very concise. Use your "I help" statement that we covered earlier in this book. Make sure that people can remember who you are and what you do. A part of branding is how people speak about who you are and what you do when you're not in the room. Branding is the story of who you are, what you do, and what you represent. Once you make connections at in-person events, make sure that you continue to follow up and engage. Don't just go to one event, and expect people to send you referrals forever. Humble yourself, check your entitlement, and build relationships that last both online and offline.

Creating a Presence Chapter Recap

- Create content in a way that works for you. You don't have to be a blogger, a YouTuber, a podcaster, etc. Just be yourself and make a few posts about your area of expertise regularly so that people know you exist when they come looking for you.
- Build a relationship online, comment on other posts, ask questions, reply, do live stream videos together, and be friendly. Soon people will go to your page to learn more about who you are and what you do.
- The strategy for how you are creating a presence will change based on where you are in your private practice. You don't have to do everything all of the time.
    - Example-To get therapy clients, network with other therapists who have a related or complementary niche. If you work with children, network with therapists who work with adults or couples with parenting issues.
    - Example-To get speaking engagements build relationships with people who hire speakers (event coordinators, conference hosts, principals, nonprofit directors)

CHAPTER 9:
SUCCESS STUDIES

Podcast Episodes #121, 122, & 123 Success Studies Series

One of my favorite things to do once a year is a success studies series. The purpose of the series is to help therapists learn to study the success of other people, not to copy what they are doing, but to learn to do what it takes to do what they do at a high level. Remember you're only seeing the highlight reel. You need to know what they had to work through, what sacrifices they made, and what challenges they had to work to overcome. That is a true success study.

There are so many gems you can glean from learning about the journeys of other people. Through watching other therapists in the field, I learned what type of practice I wanted and didn't want. I learned how to create my dream schedule. I learned what type of neighborhood I wanted to live in. I learned how I wanted to communicate who I was and what types of clients I served. I learned how to negotiate my salary and justify it with the value I was bringing to the company. I learned how to become a forever student and ask really good questions.

Learning Moment

If you can see it, you can become it. Sometimes you just need a framework to follow as your guide. People can be really good frameworks for inspiration.

Success Studies Chapter Recap

- Build a private practice around your life, not the other way around.
- You don't have to be full-time in private practice if you don't want to be.
- Take advantage of the opportunities that are available to you.
- Decide on your niche. Nothing is wrong with choosing one demographic to serve and serving them well.
- Manage your time. Set time blocks for tasks to help keep you accountable.
- Don't ever stop being a student. Continue learning about yourself, the mental health field, and how to operate the business side of private practice.

CEO Clinician Success Studies Interview

Name Lynsey Retzlaff, LCSW

Website https://www.lynseyretzlaff.com/

Facebook https://www.facebook.com/lynseyretzlaffllc

Instagram www.instagram.com/lynsey.retzlaff

Linked In https://www.linkedin.com/in/lynseyretzlaff/

Who do you serve?

Working moms

How did you decide on your niche?

I focused on areas of expertise, as I am a working mom myself. Cameisha helped narrow down my areas of expertise and brought to my attention how much I could help working mothers just from my own experiences. It made me realize how much of a superpower I have in that area as I work full-time and became an entrepreneur while raising a family.

What have you accomplished since completing the coaching program?

I have landed my first paid speaking gig with a Women's Leadership Network for a Fortune 500 company. I have been on 2 podcasts, with another one lined up. I have also recorded myself, which was a huge barrier for me due to anxiety. I have also launched my first online course for working mothers. I joined a local Chamber of Commerce and am speaking for women in a local group with my signature speech and framework.

What personal accomplishments are you most proud of? What inner transformation do you want to share with the world?

I am most proud of my ability to meet new people and put out services that overall will do good for the world. I had a dream of speaking over a year ago and had no clue how to make that happen. Due to putting myself out there (despite having fear!), I've met great people who have taught me the way. I'm naturally introverted so this was a huge accomplishment for me! The inner transformation that helped the most was the realization that my belief of being an imposter was false. I'm proving that belief wrong daily with my services and expertise.

What do you want people to know about business coaching with Cameisha?

Cameisha's coaching was transformative for my life. She gives the practical skills needed to accomplish your goals, while also challenging you to keep going. She does this with a beautiful blend of compassion, directness, and care. She provides needed support even after the program is completed because she genuinely cares about her clients' success.

CEO Clinician Success Studies Interview #2

Name Emily Dillion, LCSW, PPSC

Website https://www.wildflowermentalhealth.com/

Facebook https://www.facebook.com/wildflowermentalhealth

Instagram https://www.instagram.com/wildflower.mentalhealth/

Linked In https://www.linkedin.com/in/emilydavisdillon/

Who do you serve?

Teens, parents of teens, adults with adolescent trauma

How did you decide on your niche?

I have enjoyed working with teens and their parents in the school setting for years and have recently added the adult services. Many of my adult clients shared that they resonate with my practice because they have unresolved trauma from their teen years. I have enjoyed working with these individuals and have expanded my niche.

What have you accomplished since completing the coaching program?

The program helped me jump-start my practice. I went from barely opening my "doors" to having a full practice. I have also contracted with a therapy app as a class facilitator. I will be filming a series on teen depression/ anxiety in September. I have made many connections in my community and I am working on parenting workshops and a group curriculum.

What personal accomplishments are you most proud of? What inner transformation do you want to share with the world?

I am most proud of the confidence and self-assurance I have gained. I went from feeling on edge, anxious, and full of worry, to really owning my practice and expertise. I feel at ease as both a private practice therapist and a business owner. I even put "Therapist & CEO" as my title on Linked In. 😆

What do you want people to know about business coaching with Cameisha?

Cameisha is kind, compassionate, and authentic and will inspire and encourage you at every step of your journey. Her program is thorough and she walks you through everything using lots of tools and visuals.

CEO Clinician Success Studies Interview #3

Name Chelsea Taylor, LAC

Website https://www.chatwitchelscounseling.com

Facebook https://www.facebook.com/profile.php?id=100087789812278

Instagram www.instagram.com/chatwitchels

Linked In www.linkedin.com/in/chelsea-taylor-lac-764450140

Who do you serve?

Gen Z & Millennials: Life transitions, anxiety, & depression

How did you decide on your niche?

I relate to young people, especially college students. I help people with life transitions such as starting college, starting a new job, and the birth of a new child.

What have you accomplished since completing the coaching program?

I have had a speaking engagement at a well-known power energy company, a 2-day engagement workshop on grief and loss for a church, collabs with a community garden (I'm still trying to figure out how to mix this for profit), another speaking engagement for a church, maintaining IG page and creating content, purchased merchandise (business pens, flyers, brochure), participated in a vendor event for the city of Little Rock, bought a domain, got my business on Google, networked like a boss, and started working on a 6-week self-esteem group therapy course for teens.

What personal accomplishments are you most proud of? What inner transformation do you want to share with the world?

Taking on the speaking engagements. I questioned my worth before I started the program. I had to learn and unlearn new ways to handle money. I had to sit with myself and explore what held value to me. I stopped doubting myself when I got into this course. I gained confidence and competence when I graduated from the program. My proudest accomplishment was investing in myself.

What do you want people to know about business coaching with Cameisha?

It's worth it! This investment in yourself has unlimited possibilities.

PART 4

MOVEMENT OF A CEO CLINICIAN

CHAPTER 10:
VISION FOR THE FUTURE

Podcast Episode #105 How to Market & Lead Your Private Practice

So everyone wants to be a visionary because it's a cool trend. Typically, visionaries are people who have big dreams, big ideas, and endless creativity. They can see into the future and they can communicate what they have seen in a very compelling way. Now the challenge with visionaries is sometimes visionaries get so grandiose in their thinking that it almost comes across like cotton candy and unicorns. It's not practical at all. So as a CEO clinician who's building a private practice, building a brand, and looking to expand services, you have to be both a visionary and practical enough to communicate that vision to the people who are going to help you carry it out. If you remember when I talked to you about goals in the very beginning, your big goal is simply the summary of all of your smaller goals. So when it comes to vision for your private practice, if your goal is to make a minimum of $75,000 per year starting out, then you need to backtrack and figure out what it is going to take to get you to 75,000 per year.

You need to know how you're going to get there, who you need on your team to help you, how much will their help cost you, and what time frame you have to realistically make all those things happen.

A part of the reason I spend so much time stressing to therapists about logistics, details, mechanics, and operations is that I've seen private practices fall apart due to a lack of structure. I've seen practices plateau in their revenue because they didn't have processes in place. I've seen therapists lose thousands of dollars and have to go back to their agency or pick up a contract position because they were trying to do too much too soon and didn't have the data to support the decision to pursue the vision.

Knowing Your Numbers

Now when I say you need data to support decisions, you need to be looking at how much money you are making per session, how many sessions are you doing per week, how many clients you have that are private pay only, and how many clients you have that use insurance. Of your insurance clients, you need to know how many of them have Blue Cross Blue Shield and how many of them have United Healthcare. You need to know what your contracted reimbursement rate is for each insurance panel you are on as a provider. This will help you budget for your home and for your business. As a CEO, you need a full statistical breakdown of the ins and outs of your practice. Those numbers will guide your vision for the future. We make future decisions from current data and we follow the trends within your business, not just the trends of the external market. So looking at your data, after you have paid all of your expenses for the business, paid yourself, put money aside for taxes, and have put money aside for emergencies, now you can now make decisions with clarity for what remains. How much money do you have left over? What is the assignment you have for the remaining money? Some of you may be thinking of hiring a team member or independent contractor. If you only have $100 left at the end of the month, you may not be ready to hire someone. If one client cancels or doesn't show, then you will be in the red.

One of the most costly mistakes I made very early in my private practice was making financial decisions that I wasn't ready or in a position to make. I had a really good relationship with a therapist in my area who convinced me to get my own office space. She told me that would be the key to getting more clients. At this time, I didn't know much about marketing a private practice. I was just getting started. I trusted her as a mentor so I took her word. I rented an office space and it was about $400 a month which isn't ridiculous, but I was only seeing about two clients a week at $100 per session. I had massive overhead every month, and I still had to pay for additional things to run my practice. For the entire six months of the lease agreement, I did not make any profit. I was excited to move into the office space. I found some furniture from an online yard sale that I could afford. It was cozy and I enjoyed being there, but it was too far from the interstate for clients to conveniently get in and get out. What I did not know was that my mentor lived in the area, had children who went to school in the area, and had been practicing in the area for almost 15 years. Her recommendation was not unhelpful, but it wasn't the right time for me. I didn't have enough data to help me make an evidence-based business decision.

Looking at the data alone, I should have continued to sublease a space from someone else or remained completely virtual until I had more clients.This would cover the overhead and would still leave room for me to be able to make a profit. So the takeaway that I want you to get from this story is your numbers will tell you what your practice is ready for better than any mentor or coach ever will. Don't take my word for it, look at your numbers. What was your income at the end of last month? The next question is what can you do with that amount of money and how often is that your true profit number? If it's two or three times out of the year, you're not ready for bigger business decisions. I know that's hard for you to hear, but I care more about your success and private practice than your ears being challenged at this moment.

Now if you don't like the way your numbers look, then your options are to cut expenses or increase income to support the vision. When you are in the early stages of building your practice, hiring an intern can be a great solution to building your team at little to no cost. My recommendation is to really spend time training your intern and helping them to develop their skillset and to be a great asset to your company. Many interns are eager to learn and they simply need someone who believes in them to give them a chance and an opportunity to learn. If you need help with marketing, then recruit a marketing intern, not a social work intern or a counseling intern. Choose an intern with a knowledge base for the position.

Through coaching with me, we will evaluate and assess where your business is, and what is next on the horizon for you. We will come up with a plan of who your hires need to be, if any. If you are not in a position to hire, that means you have to do it for yourself for a little longer, and then go make more money to buy back your own time. This is how I hired my first office manager. I needed my time to be spent elsewhere. I needed to off-board myself from working in my business to working on it. When I was able to focus on being a therapist and not doing administrative work, I became a better therapist and it felt like my clients were making more progress. That was a part of the vision.

Learning Moment

What I want you to take away from this chapter is that sometimes the vision-based decisions that you have to make in private practice have nothing to do with what you see directly. Sometimes vision-based decisions happen in unrelated areas like money management, time management, or the health of your marriage. The amount of hours of sleep you're getting, the way you save and invest your money, and how hydrated you are during the day. It all matters. Private practice also carries over into every other area of your life that isn't directly a part of the practice. You need physical stamina and mental fortitude to carry the vision.

Vision & Mindset Chapter Recap

- Be a visionary and be practical enough to communicate that vision to the people who are going to help you carry it out.

- Know your numbers by using financial reporting software tools like Wave or Quickbooks to help you understand how much you're bringing in, what's going out, and what your profit margins are.
- You need physical stamina and mental fortitude to carry the vision.

CHAPTER 11:
HIRING YOUR DREAM TEAM

Podcast Episode # 110 How to Build a 6-Figure Practice

Okay friends, let's talk about hiring your dream team. Whenever you get ready to hire your dream team there are several factors you need to consider. Wait to hire your first team member until you are sure that you are ready. You may be personally ready, however, you need to make sure that the business is ready. You also need to make sure that you have a CPA on your team to help you make these financial decisions. When hiring a team member, certain documents need to be in place, and information needs to be obtained before you make this hire. You also need a contract, job description, and set of expectations, including a confidentiality agreement. Make sure the software and the tech you are using are secure, encrypted, and protected.

When you hire, you need to make sure that you can afford to pay them for at least three to six months' worth of work. Oftentimes, independent contractors require 90 days minimum to work with you. Because sometimes it takes three months to learn your systems and processes. It will take time for your new team member to become more efficient with their time. You need to plan to be very patient with your first new hire because you will have to train them on how you operate your business. You also need to be very careful because several people specifically seek out new therapists in private practice or established therapists who are not very good at business. They know they can take advantage of you and some people are just not good people. So when you're interviewing, you need to screen them and make sure they have good recommendations. Ask for samples of their work. It also wouldn't hurt to ask about their values and their beliefs to see if there is alignment.

You don't have to work with everyone. Any person who is on your team is an extension of you as CEO. They are essentially your eyes, ears, and sometimes hands in other areas. So if they show up in a way that doesn't reflect your company and your brand in a good light, then they may not be the person to hire, even though they may be good at what they do. In the business world, character and integrity will often take you further than good marketing ever will. When people have a good experience with you or someone from your team and they feel valued, they are more than likely to send referrals. They may even name-drop you for future opportunities and the opposite is also true. If they have a horrible experience with you or anyone from your team they may say really bad things about you and there's nothing you can do about it. Of course there are times when you can be good to people, provide a good customer service experience, and do your best to make sure they feel valued and appreciated while working with you and people will still leave you a really bad review online. Some people will spread rumors about you and say you are a terrible therapist no matter what. That is okay as long as there are other people singing your praises to offset your negative reviews. Negative reviews don't feel good. Believe it or not, I've had them. I've also gotten really negative feedback on surveys that we've done over the years and you just have to take it and move on. Some of the suggestions you need to pay attention to and make necessary changes.

When you're bringing on your first team member, you have to give yourself time to learn how to communicate what you need from them. Give yourself time to learn how to communicate the vision for where you are going as a company. Give them time to learn, implement, and ask questions. You also have to give them time to make mistakes. Some of the mistakes they will make will cost you time, other mistakes will cost you money. I highly recommend you put everyone on a 90-day trial period to see how they work and to determine if they are a good fit for you. How much time does it take to complete those costly tasks? Do not keep them for a day longer than you need to.

Learning Moment

The general rule for the industry is to be slow to hire and quick to fire. This is where you have to remember what I taught you earlier. Some things are not personal, it's just business. If a team member is costing you money and they're not helping you make money, it is okay to fire them. If you're stressed because of their mistakes and the money it's costing your company, you have to remove them as quickly as possible. If you choose to work with me for coaching, I will show you the behind-the-scenes of how I train my team, what systems we use, what onboarding process we use, and how I communicate tasks to them. I'll show you how I communicate the vision, check their metrics, track their performance, the type of feedback I give them, and how I celebrate my team for doing well.

Hiring Your Dream Team Chapter Recap

- Leadership is a skill you need to develop. Use books, courses, masterclasses, events, coaching programs, and your peers to help you grow.
- Be very clear on what you need each member of your team to do and how you need them to do it. Walk them through it step by step, and use Zoom videos, Loom videos, and resources like Slack to speak to them quickly.
- Save your money in advance so you can afford to hire a team member for at least three months. You may also need to have an additional three months saved up to cover their mistakes if they make one.
- Schedule coffee dates with other professionals who work in the field of human resources, recruiting, and talent management and ask them for tips, resources, and how they approach hiring new people for a company.

CHAPTER 12:
BEYOND THE BOOK

Podcast Episode #119 Being Relevant as a Therapist

Podcast Episode #106 Why You Need a Coach, not a Consultant

I want to take some time to share with you what happens beyond the book. Now I'm an educator and so yes I teach you what to do, but I'm also teaching you how to do it because the day might soon come when you will be writing your own book and sharing your story. You'll be sharing your experiences and expertise with the world. They will hear your voice. Even if you have no desire to write a book, there are still several ways you can share your story based on whatever path you choose.

Beyond this book, you have to choose your path. You have to choose what type of clinician you will be. You will have to choose what type of practice you will have. You will have to choose your style of operations, and the type of people you will serve. You will have to choose how you handle rejection, stress, fear, insecurity, crisis, tragedy, natural disaster, global pandemics, and things we don't know anything about yet.

Learning Moment

The biggest takeaway that I want you to have as the reader is to know that nothing is impossible for you. I'm very strong in my faith and I do believe that when you operate from a place of compassion, empathy, and service, good things come to you. Yes, I'm a businesswoman. I'm a business coach who teaches therapists how to make money by monetizing their skill set and expertise so that they can take care of their families and live a comfortable lifestyle. But I'm so in love with the work that I do and the people I help, that I honestly would do it for free. You may not quite be there yet. Beyond the book, you will be in a position where you have to decide what type of life you will live and what borders you will go beyond. You will have to decide which corrupt systems and social injustices will you work to dismantle.

Will you advocate for nonprofit initiatives? Will you financially support others with your time, your talents, and your resources? I talk about being an out-of-the-box therapist, but you also need to be an out-of-office therapist. You need to be visible in your community. People need to know who you are and what you do. If there's a tragedy or a disaster in the area, people need to think of you because that means that they trust your voice, your knowledge, and they know who you are and what you do. The biggest thing is they know how to get in contact with you and that has happened because of your marketing, consistency, and being visible both online and offline.

Beyond the book, I have several ways I can support you. I have several options where I can walk with you step by step into setting up your private practice, marketing your private practice, and structuring your private practice, and we can do it together in less than 60 days.

Beyond the book some of you will not do anything. Some of you will allow your negative core beliefs and limiting mindset to cripple you, and you will allow fear to be greater than the people you were called to serve. There's nothing I can do about it. Some of you will partially show up for your private practice, and some of you will continue to play small in the shadows. You might somewhat market. You will somewhat get structured or somewhat get on top of your numbers. You will settle for an okay lifestyle and that is also fine. But there are some of you who now have a stirred heart and it has reignited a fire in you. This book has given you courage and confidence. It has normalized your experiences and pushed you in ways you didn't even know you needed to be pushed. Because of that, you will never be the same. This is one of those types of books that grabs you, shakes you at your core, and agitates you to forward movement. For those of you who are ready for forward movement, I am also ready to meet you at the next step.

Dr. Todd Patten, my clinical supervisor at Harding University, said something to me I will never forget. I was stalling about taking my boards. I had anxiety and a lot of fear. I wanted to take the easy way out and be a life coach. He reminded me that I was a clinically trained counselor. He literally said to me, “If there’s any fear, go right toward it,” and this has stuck with me for all of these years because some days I don’t even know which direction to approach the fear. This book was one of them. I knew this book would challenge me. I knew it would stretch me. I knew this book would end up in the hands of people that I’ve never met and I may never meet. But I also knew that the world needed this information to be in the form of a book. I knew that there would be a therapist like you with this book in your hands who has been crying about your agency or working in an inpatient facility where you are not safe. You may have been threatened, and called names by patients and staff, and as bad as you wanted to leave and work somewhere else, you can’t afford it and you don’t have any options.

I also knew that beyond this book there would be some group practice owners who are very angry that my CEO clinician framework was being taught all across the world and there were therapists bypassing group practice structures to go out on their own. Beyond this book, I knew that there would be people saying that I was not qualified to help and they would challenge my license, credentials, my training, the color of my skin, my age, and my religious beliefs. But I decided that I would be the type of person who showed up for you in spite of all that. I know you need this. You need my course, my coaching program, and my support. But bigger than that, the world needs YOU. The world needs your heart, your talents, your gifts, your compassion, your empathy. and your creativity. The things that agitate you are the things you were created to change, mental health-related or not. You can do this! Myself and the entire Cameisha Brewer Consulting team are praying for you even now. We believe in you. We expect to see you do great things in your sphere of influence as a CEO Clinician.

So beyond the book who will you become?
What people will you help?
What problems will you solve?
What type of impact will you make?
How will the world be different if you decide to become a CEO clinician ?

Beyond the Book Chapter Recap

- Choose your own path even if you don't have all of the answers right now. You have enough information to take the next step, whatever that is for you.
- Decide what type of practice you want to have at this stage. Remember you can always change it later. Just get started.
- Decide what type of clients you will serve, how you will help them, and what will they be able to do after working with you.
- Own your place in the field of mental health.
    - Stop asking for everyone else's opinions.
    - Stop asking for feedback on EVERYTHING you create.
    - Start believing in yourself at each step of the journey.
    - Take a chance and go for it.

Thank you for reading. I pray that the words I have written will bring value to your life and move you forward. Stuck is not the end of your story.

ABOUT THE AUTHOR

As a therapist, business coach, speaker, and author, Cameisha is passionate about helping people prioritize their mental health. Whether you've heard her speak at an event or talked with her during a session, any conversation with Cameisha is intriguing and thought-provoking.

Cameisha's extraordinary story of transforming her own life from being an orphaned teen living on public assistance to becoming a successful entrepreneur with a thriving business is the inspiration behind her bold mission to teach others that with God all things are possible. Today, fans across the country admire her mission of teaching people how to build a life they love by shifting their thoughts into alignment with their goals.

Cameisha has been a special guest on numerous podcasts, journals, magazines, educational, and religious platforms.

Cameisha's Training:

B.S in Psychology

Minor Youth & Family Ministry

M.S. Clinical Mental Health Counseling

Ed.S Clinical Mental Health Counseling

Licensed Psychotherapist

National Board Certified Counselor

EPILOGUE

Support for Established Therapists Looking to Scale Available at https://www.cbrewerconsulting.com/

If you are ready to start making more money and working less in your private practice, I want you to know I see you, I hear you, and I understand the challenges you are facing. There is a brand new world that opens up after therapists are able to fill their caseload. There are more expenses, more challenges, more opportunities, and a newly formed perfect recipe for burnout and decision fatigue. Continuing down this path is mentally unhealthy and places you, your clients, and your license at risk. Do any of the following statements resonate with you?

- "I'm just not good at numbers."
- "I don't know how much to put aside for taxes."
- "I think I need a CPA at this point, but I don't even know what to look for."
- "I want to hire someone to help me because I'm overwhelmed and I can't take any more clients, but how do I hire?"
- "I still don't feel like I know what I'm doing in my practice."

- "Insert your challenge here ____________."

Therapists need support with packaging their expertise, monetizing their skills, and learning to build wealth. When I started making money in my private practice, I didn't know what to do next. I'm a businesswoman and I enjoy making money. I knew that I needed to create a product or service that would allow me to make passive income. So I wrote my first book, created an online course, created a paid membership program, and secured speaking engagements. I sold bulk book orders at events, and when I did speaking engagements, I needed to know how to untie myself from 1:1 direct care. I used what I knew, packaged it, monetized my skills, and was able to pay off debt and now I'm starting to aggressively build wealth. I've come a very long way from being a preschool teacher in a germ-infested classroom with the sweetest children you'll ever meet in your life. Please remember, it's not about where you start, it's about how you shift and impact the world as you continue on your journey of becoming who you are.

I pray you have enjoyed the words I've written. I cannot wait to meet you in the field. Believe it or not, you are well on your way to becoming a CEO Clinician.

I'll see you in the field.

Love,
Cameisha

HIRE CAMEISHA FOR A TRAINING

https://www.cbrewerconsulting.com/speaking

PRESENTATION TOPIC

"The CEO Clinician"

This training provides new clinicians with a framework that helps them not only build a strong foundation for a thriving practice but also develop a CEO mindset that will position them for mental freedom and a meaningful career.

*Perfect for graduate counseling programs.

- Mindset - Learn how to create a business mindset that helps you achieve your goals.
- Money - Learn how to price your services and sell them through the relationships you build.
- Marketing - Learn how to create an online and offline presence to attract ideal clients.
- Movement - Learn how to become a leader and build a team to help you scale your practice for the future.

*You can also purchase a bulk book order of the book *The CEO Clinician* for your audience in advance.

PRESENTATION TOPIC

"Empathy for Anxious Professional Women"

This training uses a variety of methods and strategies to help you as an individual or leader to work through anxiety, relationship problems, work-life balance, self-care, setting boundaries, and ultimately decrease anxiety.

*Perfect for corporations, businesses, staff members, and leadership teams.

*You can also purchase a bulk book order of the book, *Thought Life Confessions, Inner Conversations of Anxious Successful Women* for your audience in advance.

PRESENTATION TOPIC

"The Integration of Mental Health in Ministry"

This training helps you to understand the different aspects of mental health in marketplace ministry settings and how you can be proactive in the lives of the people you care about as well as yourself.

*Perfect for faith-based organizations, churches, and nonprofit organizations.

SYNOPSIS

Set up. Structure. Market. Scale Your Mental Health Private Practice in 60 Days!

One of the biggest gaps in the mental health industry is the lack of knowledge of the business of private practice. Somehow we completed graduate school, passed our licensure exams, went through supervision, paid our fees, and became licensed to practice, but no one taught us how to be a business owner of the practice.

Do you desire to have your own private practice but you have no idea where to start? Do you often question whether or not you have what it takes to build a business? Are you anxious about the business side of private practice? Do you struggle with having a positive mindset? Do you stress out about not knowing how to attract ideal clients and where to find them? Do you question whether or not people will pay you your full rate? Are you tired of overthinking the concept of marketing both online and offline? Are you tired of paying for directories or waiting for SEO to magically send you clients?

There is hope. There is a way for you to learn how to use relationship-based marketing as the most effective way to build your practice. It is possible for you to earn more than what you're making at your agency while working less. It is possible for you to learn how to create your own benefits so you feel financially secure in your practice. It is possible for you to attract ideal clients with ease.

In this book, I will teach you my signature CEO Clinician framework that has helped therapists across the country go from struggling with their mindset about the business of private practice with zero clients to having a full caseload with more consultations scheduled and booked speaking engagements in 60 days!

In the book *The CEO Clinician*, I will teach you about:

- Mindset - Learn how to create a business mindset that helps you achieve your goals.
- Money - Learn how to price your services and sell them through the relationships you build.
- Marketing - Learn how to create an online and offline presence to attract ideal clients
- Movement - Learn how to become a leader and build a team to help you scale your practice for the future.

As a therapist, business coach, speaker, and author, Cameisha is passionate about helping people prioritize their mental health. Whether you've heard her speak at an event or talked with her during a session, any conversation with Cameisha is intriguing and thought-provoking.

Cameisha's extraordinary story of transforming her own life from being an orphaned teen living on public assistance to becoming a successful entrepreneur with a thriving business is the inspiration behind her bold mission to teach others that with God all things are possible. Today, fans across the country admire her mission of teaching people how to build a life they love by shifting their thoughts into alignment with their goals.

For more information visit www.cbrewerconsulting.com

BONUS RESOURCES

Book Bonus Resources visit

https://www.cbrewerconsulting.com/ceoclinicianbookbonus

https://www.cbrewerconsulting.com/podcasts/the-ceo-clinician-podcast